Homemade D
Simple and Easy Recipes for Your Dog

Cathy L. Kidd

Author's Note:
To keep this book priced affordably, the pictures are in black
and white. To see them in color, (and get a surprise bonus) visit
us at:

http://luiniunlimitedpublications.com/?p=107

Table of Contents

Introduction

It is so much fun to make homemade treats for your dog! It takes less time and effort than you would think and gives you so many benefits for the time spent. Plus your dog will love you even more!

One of the main benefits is you can completely control the ingredients. You can eliminate preservatives and tailor the recipes to what your dog likes. Also, if you have a dog with food allergies, you can use substitutes for anything he can't eat.

Think of these recipes as guidelines. You can of course follow them exactly or you can use your imagination and create the perfect treat your dog will love.

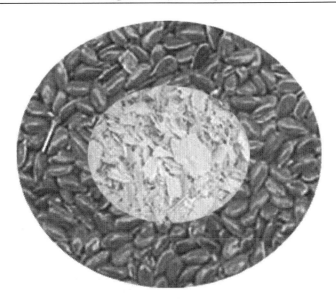

About Some of the Ingredients
in These Recipes

Bone Meal
Bone meal provides nutritional support for your dog's bones, teeth, nerves and muscles. It is a powder created by crushing the bones of animals, primarily cattle. The best manufacturers use bones from well cared for animals and sterilize the ingredients used during the manufacturing process. Some of them also test for heavy metals such as lead and aluminum to be sure the meal contains the smallest amount possible. Always be careful to read the label and research the manufacturer so you know what you're getting is of the highest quality.

Brown Rice Flour
Brown (or white) rice flour gives the biscuits crunch and promotes better digestion for your dog. Many dogs have touchy stomachs or allergies and can not, like many people I know, tolerate wheat.

Flax Seeds and Meal

Flax seeds (pictured at the start of this section) are one of the oldest foods known. They are the seeds of the flax plant and are very low carb, high nutrition with a pleasant nutty taste. They can be used whole but should be ground into meal in order to get their full nutritional benefit. A simple spice or coffee grinder can do this easily.

Health food, specialty and many regular grocery stores carry flaxseed meal as well as whole flax seeds. Whole flax seeds stay fresh for up to a year if stored safely, however flax seed meal goes bad more quickly. If you are in doubt about how long the product has been on the shelves or how it has been stored, it is recommended that you purchase whole flax seeds and grind them yourself.

Lecithin

Lecithin is found in several of the recipes in this book. Most often it is an optional ingredient. Lecithin supports the nail, hair, and skin health of your dog. There are also some studies that say it has some benefits stimulating memory and learning abilities to help with their training activities. You can get it at pharmacies, health food stores or online.

Nutritional Yeast

Nutritional yeast (pictured at the start of this section) is a kind of yeast that has been grown under controlled conditions and treated with heat so that it is no longer active. It's used as a flavor enhancer and because it is very rich in B-vitamins. For our dogs it can help with the metabolism of the fat, carbohydrate, and proteins that are critical for your dog's health. It is also a probiotic with beneficial digestive enzymes and enhances immunity.

Toxic Ingredients

Below is a list of some ingredients you should avoid when making treats for your dog. Some of them, like garlic, are fine in very small amounts and when the treats are eaten in moderation. Be aware of what you are feeding your dog and how much he is getting on a daily basis.

Alcohol
Apple Seeds (in large amounts)
Avocado
Broccoli (in large amounts)
Chives
Chocolate
Cigarettes, tobacco, cigars
Coffee and tea (caffeine)
Cooked bones, especially from fish and poultry
Corn cobs
Fruit seeds and pits
Garlic (in large amounts)
Grapes, raisins and currants
Hops (used in home brewing)
Macadamia nuts
Moldy/spoiled foods
Mushrooms
Onion
Potato peelings and green potatoes
Rhubarb leaves
Tomato leaves & stems (green parts)
Yeast dough, uncooked
Xylitol (artificial sweetener)

So make something great for your dog today and visit my Facebook page to tell us about it:

Recipes For Your Kitchen Appliances

The Recipes

Biscuits

Alfalfa Sprout

1/2 cup	Soy flour
2 cups	Whole wheat flour
2 tablespoons	Nutritional yeast
1/2 teaspoon	Salt
3 tablespoons	Alfalfa sprouts, chopped
1 tablespoon	Lecithin powder (optional)
1 teaspoon	Bone meal (optional)
1 cup	Brown rice, cooked
3 tablespoons	Canola oil
1/2 cup	Water

Preheat your oven to 350°.

Combine the flours, yeast, salt, alfalfa, lecithin and bone meal and mix well. Add the rice and oil, mixing well. Add enough of the water to form a soft but not crumbly dough.

Place the ball of dough onto a floured board and roll out to about 1/4 inch thick. Cut into small shapes with a cookie cutter and place on cookie sheets.

Bake for 25 minutes.

Apple

2 cups	Whole wheat flour
1/2 cup	All purpose flour
1/2 cup	Cornmeal
1	Apple, chopped
1	Egg, beaten
1/3 cup	Vegetable oil
1 tablespoon	Brown sugar
3/8 cup	Water

Preheat your oven to 350°. Spray cookie sheets with vegetable oil spray.

Combine the flours and cornmeal and mix well. Add the apple, egg, oil, sugar and water and mix well.

Place the ball of dough onto a floured board and roll out to about 1/2 inch thick. Cut into shapes with a cookie cutter and place on cookie sheets.

Bake 35-40 minutes. If desired, turn off the oven and leave the biscuits in for 1 hour to make them extra crisp.

Apple Cinnamon

2 cups	Dried apple
1 teaspoon	Cinnamon
1 tablespoon	Dried parsley
1 cup	Ice water
1/2 cup	Corn oil
5 cups	Flour
1/2 cup	Powdered milk
2 large	Eggs

Preheat your oven to 350°.

Put the apples in a food processor or blender and process until the pieces are small.

Combine the apples and other ingredients and mix well. Add a little more oil or water if the dough is too dry.

Place the ball of dough onto a floured board and roll out to about 1/4 inch thick. Cut into shapes with a cookie cutter and place on cookie sheets.

Bake for 20-25 minutes until golden brown.

Note: You can substitute 3/4 cup of corn meal for an equal amount of the flour if desired.

Baby Food

2 cups   Whole wheat flour
2 (4oz.) jars   Pureed baby food

Preheat your oven to 350°.

Combine the ingredients and mix well to form a stiff dough. Add extra flour or water as needed.

Place the ball of dough onto a floured board and roll out to about 1/4 inch thick. Cut into shapes with a cookie cutter and place on cookie sheets lined with parchment paper.

Bake for 20-25 minutes.

Notes: You can use beef, blueberry, sweet potato, or chicken baby food. Just be sure there are no onions, onion powder or artificial preservatives in it.

You can substitute wheat germ, spelt flour, rolled oats or a mix of flours for the whole wheat flour. This is a good recipe for dogs with allergies. Because there are only two ingredients, you can easily customize it to suit your dog.

You can also add grated carrots or sweet potatoes, a sprig of parsley (for bad breath), blueberries, or some homemade peanut butter for variety.

Barbeque

2 cups	Whole wheat flour
1/2 cup	All purpose flour
1/2 cup	Cornmeal
1/2 cup	Wheat germ
1/2 cup	Barbeque sauce
2 tablespoons	Honey
3 tablespoons	Vegetable oil
1	Egg
1/2 cup	Water

Preheat your oven to 350°.

Combine the dry ingredients in a large bowl. In a separate bowl, mix the barbeque sauce, honey, oil, egg, water. Add to dry ingredients mixing well.

Place the ball of dough onto a floured board and roll out to about 1/4 inch thick. Cut into 3-4 inch pieces and place on ungreased cookie sheets.

Bake for 25 minutes.

Note: Be sure to check the ingredient list of whatever barbeque sauce you choose for this recipe.

Beef

2 1/2 cups	Whole wheat flour
1/2 cup	Powdered milk
1/2 teaspoon	Salt
1 teaspoon	Brown sugar
6 tablespoons	Beef drippings
1	Egg, beaten
1/2 cup	Ice water

Preheat your oven to 350° and spray cookie sheets with vegetable oil spray.

Combine the flour, milk, salt, and sugar and mix well. Stir in the beef drippings mixing until the mixture has a corn meal like texture. Mix in the egg and enough water to form a ball.

Place the ball of dough onto a floured board and roll out to about 1/2 inch thick. Cut into small shapes with a cookie cutter and place on cookie sheets.

Bake for 25-30 minutes.

Beef Cheese

1/2 cup	Reduced fat cheddar cheese, shredded
3 1/2 cups	Whole wheat flour
1 cup	Beef broth
1/4 cup	Skim milk
1/2 cup	Green beans, cooked and mashed
1 tablespoon	Margarine

Preheat your oven to 350 F.

Combine the shredded cheddar cheese and flour and mix well.
Add the beef broth, skim milk, green beans and margarine and
mix to form a dough ball.

Knead the dough until smooth and roll out to 1/4 inch thick.
Cut into shapes and place on ungreased cookie sheets.

Bake for 30 minutes.

Cheese

1/4 cup	Water
2	Eggs
2 cups	All purpose flour
1 1/3 cups	Sharp cheddar cheese, shredded
3 cloves	Garlic, finely chopped
1/2 cup	Vegetable oil

Preheat your oven to 350° and spray cookie sheets with vegetable oil spray.

Combine the water and eggs in a small bowl and mix well.

Combine the flour, cheese, garlic and oil in the bowl of a food processor and pulse for about 5 seconds. Scrape the sides of bowl and pulse another 5 seconds. The mixture should have the consistency of cornmeal.

With the processor running, add the egg mixture until the dough forms a ball.

Place the ball of dough onto a floured board and roll out to about 1/4 inch thick. Cut into small shapes with a cookie cutter and place on cookie sheets.

Bake for 15 minutes. Turn each biscuit over and bake for another 10 minutes.

Chicken (Version 1)

3/4 cup	Cornmeal
1/2 cup	Vegetable oil
3 cups	Whole wheat flour
1 cup	Chicken broth

Preheat your oven to 375°.

Combine all of the ingredients and mix well.

Place the dough onto a floured board and roll out to about 1/4 inch thick. Cut into small shapes with a cookie cutter and place on cookie sheets.

Bake 30-40 minutes

Note: You can substitute beef broth for the chicken if desired.

Chicken (Version 2)

2 1/2 cups	All purpose flour
3/4 cup	Yellow cornmeal
1/4 cup	Cooked chicken, chopped
1 cup	Chicken broth
4 tablespoons	Soft margarine
1	Egg
2 tablespoons	Milk

Preheat your oven to 325°.

Combine the flour, cornmeal, chicken, broth and margarine and mix well.

Form into a soft dough and knead for 3 minutes. Place the dough onto a floured board and roll out to about 1/4 inch thick. Cut into small shapes with a cookie cutter and place on ungreased cookie sheets.

Beat the egg and milk together and apply to the top of the biscuits with a brush for a glaze.

Bake for 35 minutes.

Cilantro Parsley

1 1/4 cups	Water
4 cups	Whole wheat flour
1/2 cup	Cornmeal
1	Egg
1/4 cup	Applesauce
1/2 cup	Cheese, grated
1 tablespoon	Cilantro
1 tablespoon	Parsley

Preheat your oven to 375° and spray cookie sheets with vegetable oil spray.

Combine all of the ingredients in a large bowl and mix well.

Knead to form a stiff dough. Place the dough onto a floured board and roll out to about 1/2 inch thick. Cut into shapes with a cookie cutter and place on cookie sheets.

Bake for about 15 minutes until golden brown.

Fruity Cereal

2 1/2 cups	White corn meal (or rice flour)
1 1/2 cups	All purpose flour
1 1/2 cups	Fruity cereal flakes
3 tablespoons	Vegetable oil
2	Egg whites, beaten
1 cup	Warm chicken broth

Preheat your oven to 350° and spray cookie sheets with vegetable oil spray.

Combine the dry ingredients in a large bowl. In a separate bowl, combine the oil, eggs, and broth. Add to dry ingredients mixing well.

Place the ball of dough onto a floured board and roll out to about 1/2 inch thick. Cut into shapes with a cookie cutter and place on the cookie sheets.

Bake for 25 minutes. Turn the oven off and let them sit inside for several hours to harden. The longer you leave them, the crunchier they will become.

Note: These treats are an all-time favorite of the author and her dogs! The confetti effect created by the variety of colors in the fruity cereal makes these treats perfect for celebrations.

Cinnamon Honey Balls

2/3 cup	Whole wheat flour
1/3 cup	All purpose flour
1/2 cup	Bran
1/2 cup	Brewers yeast
1/4 cup	Wheat germ
1/2 teaspoon	Ground cinnamon
3 tablespoons	Honey
2 tablespoons	Vegetable oil
1	Egg
1/3 cup	Milk

Preheat your oven to 350°.

Combine the dry ingredients in a large bowl and mix well. In a separate bowl, beat the honey, oil, egg and milk until well mixed.

Gradually add the wet mixture to the dry to form a dough.

Form 1 inch balls and place on ungreased cookie sheets.

Bake for 15 minutes.

Peanut Butter (Version 1)

2 cups	Whole wheat flour
1 tablespoon	Baking powder
Dash	Salt
1 cup	Peanut butter
1/2 cup	Skim milk
1	Egg

Preheat your oven to 375° and spray cookie sheets with vegetable oil spray.

Combine the flour, baking powder and salt in a bowl. In a separate bowl, combine the peanut butter, milk and egg and mix well.

Add the wet mixture to the dry and mix well.

Place the dough onto a floured board and roll out to about 1/4 inch thick. Cut into shapes with a cookie cutter and place on the cookie sheets.

Bake for 20 minutes or until lightly brown.

Peanut Butter (Version 2)

2 tablespoons	Vegetable oil
1/2 cup	Peanut butter
1 cup	Water
1·1/2 cups	Whole wheat flour
1·1/2 cups	All purpose flour

Preheat your oven to 350°.

Combine the oil, peanut butter and water and mix well. Add the flours, one cup at a time, mixing well to form a dough.

Knead the dough to form a firm ball Place the dough onto a floured board and roll out to about 1/4 inch thick. Cut into shapes with a cookie cutter and place on ungreased cookie sheets.

Bake for 20 minutes.

Peanut Butter (Version 3)

3/4 cup	Unsweetened applesauce
1/4 cup	Peanut butter
1/2 cup	Honey
1	Egg
1 1/4 cups	All purpose flour
1 cup	Whole wheat flour
2 teaspoons	Baking soda
1 teaspoon	Ginger
1 teaspoon	Cinnamon
1/2 teaspoon	Ground cloves
1/2 cup	Peanuts, chopped

Preheat your oven to 350° and spray cookie sheets with vegetable oil spray.

Combine the applesauce, peanut butter, honey and egg in a bowl and mix well. In another bowl, combine the flour, baking soda and spices, reserving the peanuts for later.

Stir the dry mixture into the wet, mixing well. Drop the dough by teaspoonfuls onto the cookie sheets. Sprinkle the chopped peanuts on top and press gently with your fingers so they will stick to the top.

Bake for 8-10 minutes.

Peanut Butter (Version 4)

1/2 cup	Unsweetened applesauce
1	Egg, slightly beaten
1/2 cup	Chunky peanut butter
1 teaspoon	Vanilla
1 1/4 cups	Water
3 cups	Whole-wheat flour
1 cup	All purpose flour
1/2 cup	Cornmeal
1/2 cup	Quick-cooking oats
1/4 cup	Peanuts, chopped

Preheat your oven to 350° and spray cookie sheets with vegetable oil spray.

Combine applesauce, egg, peanut butter, vanilla and water in a large mixing bowl and mix well.

Add the rest of the ingredients and mix well to form a dough ball. Knead the dough until firm and smooth.

Place the dough onto a floured board and roll out to 1/4 inch thick. Cut into shapes with a cookie cutter and place on the cookie sheets.

Bake for 45 minutes until lightly browned.

Peanut Butter Graham

2	Eggs
1/8 cup	Vegetable oil
1/2 cup	Peanut butter
1 cup	Graham cracker crumbs
1 cup	Milk
1/4 cup	Wheat germ
1/4 cup	Natural bran cereal
1/4 cup	Cracked wheat
1/2 cup	Oats
2 cups	Whole wheat flour

Preheat your oven to 300°.

Combine all of the ingredients except the flour and mix well. Add the flour gradually, 1/2 cup at a time until the dough is stiff enough to handle and roll into small balls.

Place the dough in small balls on cookie sheets and flatten slightly with your finger.

Bake for 90 minutes, turning the biscuits over half way through. Lower your oven temperature to 225° and bake for about another 45 min. testing occasionally.

To test for doneness, take one out, let it cool and break it in half. It should be crisp and hard when done.

Peanut Butter Pumpkin (Version 1)

2 cups	Rice flour
1/2 cup	Peanut butter
1 cup	Canned pumpkin (not pie filling)
2	Eggs
1 1/2 teaspoons	Cinnamon

Preheat your oven to 350°.

Combine all of ingredients and mix well. Place the dough onto a floured board and roll out to 1/4 inch thick. Cut into shapes with a cookie cutter and place on cookie sheets.

Bake for 10-15 minutes.

Peanut Butter Pumpkin (Version 2)

3 cups	Whole wheat flour
1/2 cup	Oats
1/2 teaspoon	Cinnamon (optional)
2	Eggs
1 cup	Canned pumpkin (not pie filling)
3 tablespoons	Peanut butter

Preheat your oven to 350°.

Combine the flour, oats, and cinnamon in a large bowl.

In a separate bowl, combine the eggs, pumpkin and peanut butter mixing well until combined. Stir the wet ingredients into the dry to form a dough ball.

Place the dough onto a floured board and roll out to 1/2 inch thick. Cut into shapes with a cookie cutter and place on cookie sheets.

Bake for 30-35 minutes until golden brown.

Notes: You can substitute brown rice or gluten free flour for the whole wheat if desired.

Peanut Butter Sweet Potato

1 medium	Sweet potato, peeled, cubed
	Water
1/2 cup	Natural peanut butter, no sugar added
1 cup	Oat flour
1 cup	Brown rice flour
2 teaspoons	Baking powder

Simmer the sweet potato in a small pan with enough water to cover. Cook until soft. Set aside the cooking liquid and let cool.

Preheat your oven to 375°.

In a large bowl, mash the cooked sweet potato. Add 1/2 cup of the reserved liquid and the peanut butter.

In a separate bowl, combine the flours and baking powder mixing well. Add sweet potato/peanut butter mixture and mix well to form a dough ball.

Place the dough onto a floured board and roll out to 1/4 inch thick. Cut into shapes with a cookie cutter and place on cookie sheets.

Bake for 30 minutes or until medium golden brown.

Pineapple

1 (8 oz.) can	Unsweetened crushed pineapple, drained
1/2 cup	Applesauce
1	Egg
1 teaspoon	Vanilla
1 cup	All purpose flour
1 cup	Whole wheat flour
1 1/2 teaspoons	Baking powder
1/4 teaspoon	Baking soda

Preheat your oven to 350° and spray cookie sheets with vegetable oil spray.

Combine the pineapple, applesauce, egg and vanilla in a large bowl and mix well. Combine the flour, baking powder and baking soda in a separate bowl.

Add the dry mixture into the wet and mix well. Drop by tablespoonfuls onto the cookie sheets

Bake for 20 minutes.

Pumpkin

2	Eggs
1/2 cup	Canned pumpkin (not pie filling)
1/2 teaspoon	Salt
2 tablespoons	Powdered milk
2 1/2 cups	Whole wheat flour
	Water

Preheat your oven to 350°.

Combine the eggs and pumpkin and mix well. Add the salt, powdered milk, and flour. Add just enough water to make a dry and stiff dough.

Place the dough onto a floured board and roll out to 1/2 inch thick. Cut into shapes with a cookie cutter and place 1 inch apart on cookie sheets.

Bake for 20 minutes on one side, then turn the biscuits over and bake another 20 minutes.

Notes: You can substitute rice flour for the whole wheat and add a teaspoon of dried parsley if desired.

Vegetarian (Version 1)

1 1/2 cup	Water
3 tablespoons	Corn oil
2 cups	Whole wheat flour
1 1/2 cups	All purpose flour
1/2 cup	Cornmeal
1/2 cup	Celery, diced
1/8 cup	Red bell peppers, diced
1/2cup	Carrots, shredded
1 clove	Garlic, minced

Preheat your oven to 350°.

Combine the water and oil. Add the flour, cornmeal, vegetables and garlic and mix well to form a dough.

Knead the dough for 2-3 minutes. Place the dough onto a floured board and roll out to 1/4 inch thick. Cut into 3-4 inch pieces place on ungreased cookie sheets.

Bake for 30 minutes.

Vegetarian (Version 2)

2 1/2 cups	Flour
3/4 cup	Powdered Milk
1/2 cup	Vegetable oil
2 tablespoons	Brown sugar
3/4 cup	Vegetable Broth
1/2 cup	Carrots
1	Egg (optional)

Preheat your oven to 300°.

Combine all of the ingredients and mix well to form a dough ball. Place the dough onto a floured board and roll out to 1/4 inch thick. Cut into shapes with a cookie cutter and place on ungreased cookie sheets.

Bake for 30 minutes.

Whole Wheat

1/3 cup	Margarine, softened
3 cups	Whole wheat flour
3/4 cup	Milk
1	Egg
1/4 teaspoon	Garlic powder

Preheat your oven to 325° and spray cookie sheets with vegetable oil spray.

Combine the margarine and flour and mix well. In a separate bowl, combine the milk, egg and garlic powder.

Slowly add the wet mixture into the dry, mixing well to create a dough ball.

Place the ball of dough onto a floured board and roll out to about 1/4 inch thick. Cut into small shapes with a cookie cutter and place on cookie sheets.

Bake for 50 minutes.

Bread Machine Biscuits

These recipes make use of your bread machine to mix the dough. Much easier on your hands! They are also made with yeast dough so they will come out puffier than standard biscuits.

Most bread machines have a dough cycle. It will go through the following steps: kneading, first rise, punch down, and second/final rise. Leave the dough in the machine until the cycle completely finishes and the machine beeps. It can take up to an hour and a half, longer than you would think! So be patient and don't take it out too soon.

If your machine does not have a dough cycle, monitor the progress of the dough and take it out before it starts to bake.

For all of these recipes, check the dough for the first 5-15 minutes of the cycle. It should be a firm, round ball. Add flour or water if necessary.

Beef Bacon

1/2 cup	Whole wheat flour
2 cups	All purpose flour
1/2 cup	Cornmeal
1/2 cup	Oats, uncooked
1/4 cup	Oat bran
1 tablespoon	Brown sugar
1/2 teaspoon	Salt
1 cup	Beef broth
1 tablespoon	Bacon fat
1	Egg
2 tablespoons	Brewers yeast
1 tablespoon	Parsley flakes
1 1/2 teaspoons	Rapid or instant yeast
3 strips	Bacon, cooked crisp, crumbled

Cook the bacon first and reserve 1 tablespoon of the fat.

Place all of the ingredients except the bacon in the bread machine pan and set on the dough cycle. Once the dough is firm, add the bacon.

When the machine beeps, remove the dough and place it onto a board lightly dusted with cornmeal and roll out to 1/4 inch thick. Cut into shapes with a cookie cutter and place on nonstick cookie sheets.

Preheat your oven to 325°.

Bake for 45-55 minutes. Turn the oven off and let them sit inside for several hours to harden.

Beef Rice

1/2 cup	Whole wheat flour
2 1/2 cups	All-purpose flour
1/4 cup	Rice bran
3 tablespoons	Cornmeal
3 tablespoons	Powdered milk
1/2 teaspoon	Salt
3 tablespoons	Brewers yeast
1/2 teaspoon	Ground ginger
1/2 cup	Cooked rice
3/4 cup	Beef broth
1	Egg
2 tablespoons	Vegetable oil
1 tablespoon	Maple syrup
1 1/2 teaspoons	Rapid or instant yeast

Place all of the ingredients in the bread machine pan and set on the dough cycle.

When the machine beeps, remove the dough and place it onto a board lightly dusted with flour and roll out to 1/4 inch thick. Cut into shapes with a cookie cutter and place on nonstick cookie sheets.

Preheat your oven to 325°.

Bake for 45-50 minutes. Turn the oven off and let them sit inside for several hours to harden.

Broth (Version 1)

3/4 cup	Beef, chicken, or vegetable broth
1	Egg
3 tablespoons	Oil
1 cup	All purpose flour
3/4 cup	Whole wheat flour
1/3 cup	Bulgur
1/3 cup	Wheat germ
1/3 cup	Bran
1/4 cup	Powdered milk
1/4 teaspoon	Garlic powder
1 1/2 teaspoons	Yeast

Place all of the ingredients in your bread machine pan and select the dough cycle.

When the machine beeps, remove the dough and place it onto a floured board and roll out to 1/4 inch thick. Cut into shapes with a cookie cutter and place on greased cookie sheets.

Preheat your oven to 325°.

Bake for 30 minutes until brown and firm.

Notes: This amount of dough is for 1 1/2 pound bread machines.

Instead of placing the biscuits on greased cookie sheets you can sprinkle the sheets with cornmeal.

Broth (Version 2)

1 cup	Beef, chicken, or vegetable broth
1 cup	Bread or all purpose flour
1 cup	Whole wheat or rye flour
1 cup	Bulgur wheat
1/4 cup	Powdered milk
1/2 teaspoon	Salt
1 1/2 teaspoon	Yeast

Place all of the ingredients in your bread machine pan and select the dough cycle.

When the machine beeps, remove the dough and place it onto a floured board and roll out to 1/4 inch thick. Cut into shapes with a cookie cutter and place on greased cookie sheets.

Preheat your oven to 325°.

Bake for 45 minutes until done. Turn the oven off and let them sit inside for several hours to harden.

Note: This is the recipe pictured at the start of the Biscuit section.

Carrot Potato

1 cup	Whole wheat flour
1 cup	All purpose flour
1/2 cup	Yellow cornmeal
2 tablespoons	Potato flakes
2 tablespoons	Brewers yeast
1/2 teaspoon	Salt
1 tablespoons	Parsley flakes
3/4 cup	Vegetable broth
1 1/2 tablespoons	Sunflower oil
1 1/2 tablespoons	Honey
1/2 cup	Grated carrot
1 1/2 teaspoons	Rapid or instant yeast

Place all of the ingredients in the bread machine pan and set on the dough cycle.

When the machine beeps, remove the dough and place it onto a board lightly dusted with cornmeal and roll out to 1/4 inch thick. Cut into shapes with a cookie cutter and place on nonstick cookie sheets.

Preheat your oven to 325°.

Bake for 40-50 minutes.

Maple Walnut

2 cups	Whole wheat flour
1/3 cup	Cornmeal
1/3 cup	Oat bran flakes
2 tablespoons	Vital gluten (optional)
2 tablespoons	Brewers yeast
1/2 teaspoon	Salt
3/4 teaspoon	Cinnamon
3/4 cup	Water
1 1/2 tablespoons	Walnut oil
1 1/2 tablespoons	Maple syrup
1 1/2 teaspoons	Rapid or instant yeast

Place all of the ingredients in the bread machine pan and set on the dough cycle.

When the machine beeps, remove the dough and place it onto a board lightly dusted with flour and roll out to 1/4 inch thick. Cut into shapes with a cookie cutter and place on nonstick cookie sheets.

Preheat your oven to 325°.

Bake for 45-55 minutes.

Soft Pretzels

1 cup	Water
2 teaspoons	Sugar
1/2 teaspoon	Salt
1 1/4 cups	Whole wheat flour
1 1/2 cups	All purpose flour
1 teaspoon	Baking soda
1/2 cup	Flax seed meal
1 1/2 teaspoons	Rapid or instant yeast

– Optional Wash–
1 egg beaten with 1 tablespoon of water

–Optional Topping–
Whole flax seeds

Place all of the ingredients in the bread machine pan and set on the dough cycle.

When the machine beeps, remove the dough and place it onto a board lightly dusted with cornmeal and roll out to 1/4 inch thick. Roll the dough into ropes and form pretzels. Place on nonstick cookie sheets. Brush each one with the wash and top with whole flax seeds if desired.

Preheat your oven to 325°.

Bake for 40-50 minutes.

Note: For soft pretzels, remove from the oven when they are done. For hard pretzels, turn the oven off and let them sit inside for several hours.

Vegetable Bran

1 cup	Vegetable broth
1 1/2 tablespoons	Vegetable oil
1 1/2 tablespoons	Maple syrup
1/2 teaspoon	Salt
1 cup	Whole wheat flour
1 cup	All purpose flour
1/3 cup	Wheat and barley cereal or bran cereal
3 tablespoons	Wheat germ
1/3 cup	Oats, uncooked
1/3 cup	White cornmeal
2 tablespoons	Powdered milk
2 tablespoons	Brewers yeast
1 1/4 teaspoons	Rapid or instant yeast

Place all of the ingredients in the bread machine pan and set on the dough cycle.

When the machine beeps, remove the dough and place it onto a board lightly dusted with cornmeal and roll out to 1/4 inch thick. Cut into shapes with a cookie cutter and place on nonstick cookie sheets.

Preheat your oven to 325°.

Bake for 45-55 minutes.

Yogurt Cheese

3/4 cup	All purpose flour
1/2 cup	Whole wheat flour
2/3 cups	Cornmeal
1/3 cup	Oat bran flakes
1/2 teaspoon	Salt
2 tablespoons	Brewers yeast
1 tablespoon	Parsley, dried
3/4 cup	Yogurt, room temperature
1/3 cup	Cheddar cheese, grated
1 1/2 tablespoons	Vegetable oil
1 1/2 tablespoons	Barley malt syrup
1 1/2 teaspoon	Rapid or instant yeast

Place all of the ingredients in the bread machine pan and set on the dough cycle.

When the machine beeps, remove the dough and place it onto a board lightly dusted with flour or cornmeal and roll out to 1/4 inch thick. Cut into shapes with a cookie cutter and place on nonstick cookie sheets.

Preheat your oven to 325°.

Bake for 40-50 minutes.

Dehydrated Treats

All of these recipes call for a dehydrator. You can use any kind of dehydrator you like, or if you don't have one, you can make these treats in your oven.

To make them in your oven, turn your oven on to the lowest possible setting. Place the treats on non-stick baking trays on the oven racks. Prop the oven door open about two to three inches. You can use a folded kitchen towel to do this. Propping the door open allows a little air circulation to keep the oven temperature and humidity low.

Dry the treats to the desired consistency. They may take longer than they would in a dehydrator so be sure to make them when you can monitor their progress.

All of these treats should be stored in an airtight container in the refrigerator.

Applesauce Chicken

2 cups	Chicken, cooked, finely chopped
1/2	Banana
1/2 cup	Fresh spinach, finely chopped
1/2 cup	Unsweetened applesauce, no cinnamon

Combine all of the ingredients in a blender or food processor and process until smooth. It should be a thick paste consistency.

Spoon the mixture onto your dehydrator trays and dry for 3-5 hours until completely dry. The outside should be dry and the inside soft.

Bacon Chicken

2 large	Boneless chicken breasts, cooked
2 tablespoons	Bacon, cooked and crumbled
2 tablespoons	Sunflower seeds, hulled, roasted
2 tablespoons	Dry Parmesan cheese
2 tablespoons	Flour (wheat, rice, oat or barley)

Slice the cooked chicken breasts into 1/4 to 1/2 inch slices.

Combine the bacon, seeds, cheese and flour in a food processor or blender and process to a fine powder. Put the powder in a pie pan or on a large plate.

Dampen the chicken slices with a little water and coat them with the dry mixture. Press the chicken into the mixture slightly so it will coat evenly. Coat both sides.

Put the strips on your dehydrator trays and dry for 3-5 hours until completely dry. When done, the strips should break easily.

Beef Strips

2 cups	Water
1 pound	Flank steak
1 teaspoon	Ground sage
1 tablespoon	Beef bouillon, dry

Put the steak and water in a large frying pan and cook over a low heat. Sprinkle the meat with the sage and beef bouillon.

Let the meat simmer until it is thoroughly cooked. Remove the meat, letting it drain and cut into long strips. Kitchen scissors do this well.

Put the strips on your dehydrator trays and dry for 3-5 hours until completely dry.

Notes: These treats can also be frozen.

You can use stew beef or roast trimming if desired to make small pieces of meat instead of strips.

Be sure the bouillon you use has no added ingredients, especially no onion. If you want, you can omit the bouillon and/or the sage.

Beef and Cheese

2 cups	Beef, cubed to about 1/2 inch square
1 cup	Water
1/2 cup	Green vegetables, finely chopped
2/3 cup	Whole wheat flour
1/2 cup	Feta cheese, crumbled
1 tablespoon	Beef bullion
1/2 teaspoon	Ground sage

Put the beef and water in a large frying pan and simmer over a low heat until well done. Let cool.

Put the cooked beef in a food processor or blender with one cup of the water you cooked it in. Process until smooth.

Combine the meat mixture with the remaining ingredients in a large bowl. Mix well.

Spoon the mixture onto your dehydrator trays and dry 5-7 hours or until completely dry outside. They will be soft inside.

Notes: These treats can also be frozen.

For the green vegetables you can use broccoli, green beans or spinach.

Be sure the bouillon you use has no added ingredients, especially no onion. If you want, you can omit the bouillon and/or the sage.

You can substitute grated cheddar cheese for the feta and grated carrots for the green vegetables.

Cheese

1/4 cup	Cornmeal
2 cups	Whole wheat flour
3/4 cup	Water
1	Egg
1 cup	Cheese
3/4 cup	Parmesan cheese

Combine all of the ingredients except Parmesan cheese in a large bowl. Mix the dough until well combined and knead it until the dough is elastic.

Place the ball of dough onto a floured board and roll out to about 1/4 inch thick. Cut into cookies with a small cookie cutter. Dust with Parmesan cheese.

Put the cookies on your dehydrator trays and dry for 4-5 hours until completely dry.

Dehydrated Dog Food

Frozen, raw dog food, thawed or canned dog food

Start with the frozen raw or canned dog food of your choice from your local store. Form it into small patties, squeezing out any extra liquid so it will dry quicker.

Put the patties on your dehydrator trays and dry for about 4 hours until you reach the consistency your dog likes. It can be chewy like jerky or crisp like cookies.

Notes: This is what is pictured at the start of this section. It's great broken into small pieces for treats or served whole for dinner. It's a good alternative to commercial treats if you are concerned about your dog's weight.

Fruit and Vegetable

2 vegetable	Bouillon cubes
3/4 cup	Boiling water
2 3/4 cups	Whole wheat flour
3/4 cup	Powdered milk
1/2 cup	Vegetable oil
2/3 cup	Carrots, beans, apples, or blueberries
1	Egg (optional)

Dissolve the bouillon in the boiling water.

Combine all of the ingredients in a large bowl until well mixed.

Place the ball of dough onto a floured board and roll out to about 1/4 inch thick. Cut into cookies with a small cookie cutter.

Put the cookies on your dehydrator trays and dry for 6-8 hours until completely dry.

Note: You can use just about any fruit or vegetable your dog likes.

Jerky Sticks

1 pound	Ground beef
1/2 cup	Canned red kidney beans
1 cup	Zucchini, fresh, chopped
1/2 cup	Applesauce
1/2 teaspoon	Ground sage

In a skillet, cook the ground beef until completely cooked throughout. Break up any chunks so it is crumbled when done.

Drain the liquid from kidney beans and set aside. Put the beans and zucchini in food processor or blender and process until you get a smooth, thick paste.

Add the meat, applesauce and sage and process again. If the mixture is too thick, add a little of the reserved liquid from beans. The mixture is done when there are no chunks of meat or beans and it is not too wet.

Put the round tip on your jerky maker gun and fill it with the mixture. Press out four inch long treats directly on your dehydrator trays.

Dry for 3-5 hours until completely dry.

Meat

1 cup	Cooked meat, shredded
1/3 cup	Water
1/2 cup	Oatmeal
1/2 cup	Oat bran flour

Put the meat and water in a food processor or blender and process until smooth. If it's too thick to process, add more water a little at a time.

Combine the meat mixture with the oatmeal and flour in a bowl and mix to form a stiff dough ball. Knead the dough until elastic.

Place the ball of dough onto a floured board and roll out to about 1/4 inch thick. Cut into cookies with a small cookie cutter.

Put the cookies on your dehydrator trays and dry for 3-4 hours until completely dry.

Note: This recipe is a good use for any leftover meat you may have. You can use a combination of chicken, turkey, beef, or bacon.

Peanut Butter

2 cups	Whole wheat flour
1/2 cup	Cornmeal
1/2 cup	Oats
1 2/3 cups	Water
1/3 cup	Vegetable oil
1 teaspoon	Vanilla
3 tablespoons	Natural peanut butter (no added sugar)

In a large bowl, combine the whole wheat flour, cornmeal, and oats. Stir in the water, oil, vanilla and peanut butter.

Mix the dough until well combined and knead it until the dough is elastic. Add more flour or water if necessary to get the right consistency.

Place the ball of dough onto a floured board and roll out to about 1/4 inch thick. Cut into cookies with a small cookie cutter.

Put the cookies on your dehydrator trays and dry for 7-8 hours until completely dry.

Pumpkin

1 cup	Canned pumpkin (not pie filling)
1 cup	Water
1/2 cup	Oil
2	Eggs
2 cups	Whole wheat flour
1/2 cup	Cornmeal
1/2 cup	Oats
2 teaspoons	Cinnamon

Combine the pumpkin, water, oil and eggs and mix well.

In another bowl, combine the dry ingredients and mix well.

Add the dry mixture to the wet and form into a ball. Place the ball of dough onto a floured board and roll out to about 1/4 inch thick. Shape the dough into bars, squares or cut out with a small cookie cutter.

Put the treats on your dehydrator trays and dry for 6-8 hours until completely dry and crisp.

Pumpkin Chews

2 cups   Canned pumpkin (not pie filling)

Thickly spread the pumpkin on fruit roll sheets on your dehydrator trays. Dry for 6-8 hours until it is no longer sticky. Cool and cut the treats into strips.

Note: The thicker the pumpkin is on the trays, the better the treat will be. Don't be stingy!

Sweet Potato Chews

Sweet potatoes, peeled

Cut the sweet potato into 1/4" slices or strips.

Put the slices on your dehydrator trays and dry for 6-8 hours until chewy or crisp depending on the consistency your dog likes better.

Turkey and Sweet Potato

1 cup	Water
2 cups	Cooked turkey
1 cup	Sweet potato, cooked until soft
1 tablespoon	Molasses
1 1/2 cups	Old fashioned oatmeal (not cooked)
3 dozen	Cranberries, fresh or frozen (optional)

Cut the turkey into small pieces and put it with the water in a food processor or blender. Process until it is a smooth, thick paste consistency with no meat chunks.

Add the sweet potato and molasses and process again.

Pour the mixture into a large bowl and add the oatmeal. Mix well to form a soft dough. If it is too wet, add a little more oatmeal.

Spoon the dough onto your dehydrator trays and if desired, put a cranberry on top of each one, pressing slightly so it will stay.

Dry 4-5 hours or until completely dry but not crispy.

Note: You can substitute blueberries for the cranberries and white potatoes for the sweet potatoes if desired.

Walnut Peanut Chicken

2 cups	Chicken, cooked and diced
1 cup	Water
1 cup	Zucchini or summer squash, grated
1/4 cup	Flaxseeds
1 tablespoon	Unsalted peanuts
1 tablespoon	Walnuts
1 cup	Rice flour

Combine the cooked chicken and water in a food processor or blender. Process until it is a smooth, thick paste consistency with no meat chunks. Pour it into a bowl, set aside and clean the processor/blender.

Combine the flaxseeds, peanuts and walnuts in the food processor or blender and process until the pieces are small.

Add the nut mixture, squash, and rice flour to the meat mixture and mix well.

Spoon the mixture onto the dehydrator trays and dry 5-7 hours or until the outside is dry. The inside should be soft.

Note: For variety you can substitute turkey for the chicken and potato flour for the rice flour.

Whole Wheat Honey

2 2/3 cups	Whole wheat flour
1/2 cup	Powdered milk
6 tablespoons	Butter, melted
1 teaspoon	Lecithin powder
3 teaspoons	Honey
1	Egg, beaten
2/3 cup	Cold water

Combine the flour, milk, butter, lecithin and honey and mix well. Add the egg and water and mix to form a ball of dough.

Place the ball of dough onto a floured board and roll out to about 1/4 inch thick. Cut into cookies with a small cookie cutter.

Put the cookies on your dehydrator trays and dry for 6-8 hours until completely dry.

Frozen Treats

Most of these treats are frozen in ice cube trays for convenient small treats you can give your dog on special occasions. You can use any ice cube tray, but for fun, you can get special bone shaped trays or another shape.

Peanut Butter Banana (Version 1)

3 tablespoons	Natural peanut butter, no sugar added
2	Ripe bananas, mashed
1 (24 oz.) container	Low fat vanilla yogurt
2 tablespoons	Unsweetened plain applesauce (optional)

Melt the peanut butter in a microwave. Combine all of the ingredients and mix well. Freeze in ice cube trays.

Note: This is the recipe pictured above.

Peanut Butter Banana (Version 2)

1	Banana
1/2 cup	Peanut butter
1/4 cup	Oats

Combine the banana and peanut butter. Stir in the oats. Chill 1 hour. Spoon into ice cube trays and freeze.

Carrot

2	Carrots, finely grated
2 cups	Plain non-fat yogurt
1 teaspoon	Unsweetened applesauce, no cinnamon

Combine all of the ingredients and mix well. Freeze in ice cube trays.

Tuna Yogurt

1 (8oz.) can	Tuna in water
2 (32 oz.) cartons	Plain or vanilla yogurt
2 teaspoons	Garlic power
24 (3 oz.)	Plastic cups (not paper)

Combine the yogurt, tuna and garlic in a bowl and mix well. Spoon the mixture into individual plastic cups and freeze overnight.

Notes: You can add brewers yeast and/or a mashed banana for an added health boost. You can also mix in cooked peas or other vegetables.

You can substitute canned chicken for the tuna.

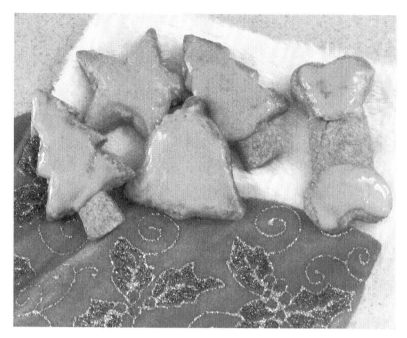

Holiday Treats

The easiest way to make festive treats for holidays and special occasions is to make any of the biscuit recipes in this book and use holiday themed cookie cutters. For an added touch you can frost them with appropriately colored icing. You can get a set of cookie cutters for every occasion and top them with one of the recipes in the Icing and Frosting section.

The Fruity Cereal biscuits earlier in this book are great for birthdays, graduation from training class or other celebrations. They come out looking like confetti and are a big hit.

For Thanksgiving you can make the Turkey and Sweet Potato dehydrator recipe. And for Christmas, there's a recipe for Candy Canes on the next page.

Happy Holidays!

Candy Cane

1 cube	Chicken bouillon
1 cup	Warm water
2 large	Eggs
3 cups	All purpose flour
1/2 cup	Powdered milk
1/2 teaspoon	Baking powder
2 teaspoons	Red food coloring

In a small bowl, dissolve the bouillon in the warm water. When dissolved, stir in the eggs.

Combine the flour, milk and baking powder in a large bowl. Stir in the bouillon mixture and mix well to form a dough ball. Knead the dough for about two minutes adding more flour if necessary so it is not sticky. Divide the dough into two balls.

Form a well in one of the balls of dough and add the food coloring. Knead the dough to thoroughly mix in the coloring and flavor. Use food safe plastic gloves when you do this!

Chill the dough in the refrigerator for 2 hours or in the freezer for 30 minutes.

Preheat the oven to 350° and spray cookie sheets with vegetable oil spray.

Divide each ball of dough into tablespoon sized balls and roll each ball into a rope to about 5 inches long. Twist one plain rope with a red strip and curl one end to form a candy cane.

Bake for 10 minutes.

Note: You can color the second ball of dough green if you want or divide the dough into 4 parts to make some red, some green canes.

Icing and Frosting

You can use these recipes to decorate the biscuit and muffin recipes in this book for special occasions.

Some of these recipes call for food coloring. In moderation, human grade food coloring is fine for dogs. However if you prefer, you can use vegetables and fruits for natural coloring. Try turmeric for yellow, avocado for green, carrots for orange, beet juice for red, and raspberries, blackberries and blueberries.

Another alternative is to get "store bought" icings that are fool proof. You can get icing from K9Cakery.com and Pastries 4 Pets. K9 Cakery also has all sorts of cool baking pans, muffin papers and party supplies.

Carob Icing

3 tablespoons	Coconut or vegetable oil
1/2 cup	Carob chips
4 tablespoons	Honey
1/4 cup	Rice almond or soy milk

Combine all of the ingredients in a small saucepan and slowly heat on the stove at medium low heat. Stir continuously with a wooden spoon.

Place cool treats on a cookie sheet lined with parchment paper. Drizzle the icing over the treats to create patterns, or dip one end in the saucepan to coat it and place it on the lined cookie sheet. Refrigerate to harden.

Egg Wash Icing

1	Egg yolk
1/4 teaspoon	Water
2-3 drops	Food coloring

Combine the egg yolk and water in a small bowl and whisk to mix well. Stir in the food coloring.

Spread the icing on uncooked dog treats using a pastry or small paint brush.

Bake the biscuits as directed.

Note: This recipe is different in that you bake the biscuit with the icing applied. It will give the biscuit a glazed, colorful look.

Honey Icing

1 teaspoon	Honey
2 teaspoons	Water
2 tablespoons	Cornstarch
3-5 drops	Food coloring of your choice

Combine the ingredients in a large mixing bowl and mix well until you have a cake frosting consistency.

Spread the icing on cool treats and refrigerate to harden.

Notes: You can substitute rice or potato flour for the cornstarch if your dog is allergic to corn. Also be aware this hardens fast! Add more water a little at a time so you can spread it on the cookies.

This is the recipe used in the picture at the start of the Holiday Treats section.

Cream Cheese Frosting

| 8 ounces | Low fat cream cheese, softened |
| 1/4 cup | Applesauce, unsweetened |

Combine both ingredients with a hand mixer until well mixed. Frost cooled muffins with a knife or use a pastry bag for more fancy decorating.

Note: You can add 2-3 drops of food coloring if desired.

Cream Cheese Honey Frosting

8 ounces	Low fat cream cheese
2 tablespoons	Honey
2 tablespoons	Plain yogurt
3 tablespoons	All purpose flour

Combine the cream cheese, honey and yogurt and mix with a hand mixer until smooth.

Mix in one tablespoon of flour at a time until you have the right consistency for spreading.

Note: You can use any type of flour for this recipe but be aware that if you use wheat flour it may affect the end color of the icing.

You can add 2-3 drops of food coloring if desired.

Yogurt Frosting

| 4 ounces | Plain yogurt |
| 2-4 tablespoons | Peanut Butter |

Combine the yogurt and peanut butter and mix well. If the mixture is too thick, add a little canola oil. If it is too thin, add a little cornstarch or flour. You want a cake frosting type consistency.

Spread the frosting on cooled treat and place them in the refrigerator to set.

Notes: You can use 2 tablespoons of honey instead of the peanut butter if desired.

The frosting will not harden completely. It will be slightly soft to the touch.

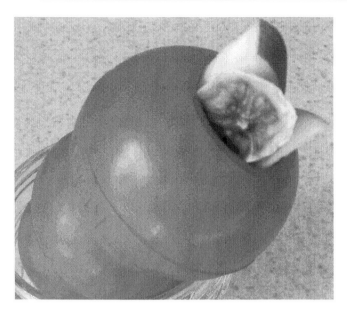

Kong Stuffing Recipes

Kongs are terrific toys that can keep your dog happily occupied for several hours. It's best to introduce them to your dog early in life so they will enjoy working on getting the treats out.

Be sure you get the right sized Kong for the size and age of your dog and if he's a heavy chewer, get the heavy duty kind. It's always a good idea to keep an eye on him the first few times he has one to be sure he eats only what's inside and not the Kong itself! You don't need a trip to the emergency vet…

Some of the recipes use soft ingredients like yogurt so a good tip to make filling the Kong easier is to place it in a mug with the small end down. This will hold it upright while you spoon the filling into the larger top end.

Also the quantities of the ingredients are just suggestions and you'll notice some of the recipes don't even have quantities. Adjust the amounts you use of each ingredient to suit your dog's tastes and the size of the Kong.

Apple

	Low fat yogurt
4-5 small pieces	Apple
3-4 slices	Banana
1 teaspoon	Peanut Butter

Place a small piece of apple in the small end of the Kong to seal it. Fill the Kong about 1/4 full with yogurt. Add a couple more pieces of apple and a couple banana slices. Add more yogurt, more apple and banana to fill. Add the peanut butter on top.

Note: This is the one pictured at the start of this section.

Applesauce Banana

Unsweetened applesauce
Bananas
Oatmeal, plain, cooked
Peanut butter
Low fat yogurt

Combine all of the ingredients, mix well and fill the Kong.

Beef Egg

Egg, scrambled
Beef, shredded
Low fat yogurt
Cheese, shredded
Mashed potatoes

Combine all of the ingredients, mix well and fill the Kong.

Blueberry Banana

Handful   Blueberries
1   Banana
                   Low fat yogurt

Mash the banana and blueberries. Add the yogurt and mix well.
Fill the Kong and place it in the freezer. Serve when frozen.

Cheese

Hard cheese, cut in pieces
Dry dog food

Combine the ingredients in a microwave safe bowl. Microwave
on high until the cheese melts. Let the mixture cool completely.
Fill the Kong and freeze.

Note: You can use cheese spread instead of the hard cheese if
you want. It won't need to be microwaved as long.

Cottage Cheese

A portion of your dog's normal kibble
1 tablespoon   Cottage cheese
1 large piece   Banana

Fill the Kong half full with kibble, then spoon in most of the
cottage cheese. Hold your hand over the large opening and
shake the Kong to coat the kibble with the cottage cheese. Add
some more kibble, packing it in well and top with the
remainder of the cottage cheese. Plug the large opening with
the banana.

Cream Cheese

A portion of your dog's normal kibble
Cream cheese

Combine the kibble with the cream cheese, mix well, and fill the Kong.

Note: You could use biscuit crumbs instead of the kibble.

Egg Hot Dog

1   Egg, scrambled, cooled
1   Hot-dog, chopped
            White rice, cooked

Mash the scrambled egg and rice together in a bowl and mix in the hot dog, reserving one larger piece. Place the larger hot dog piece in first to plug the small end and fill the Kong with the mixture.

Beef Jerky

            Peanut butter
            Chicken broth
1 stick   Beef jerky

Seal the small hole of the Kong with the peanut butter. Fill it with the chicken broth. Place a stick of beef jerky inside and freeze.

Notes: Instead of commercial human jerky, you can use dog jerky treats or pieces of steak or roast beef.

As it defrosts, it can get very messy so you may want to serve this one outside!

Freeze Dried Powder

Freeze dried food powder
Water

Soak the food powder in enough water to rehydrate. Don't let it get too wet. Fill the Kong and serve right away or refrigerate it for later.

Note: This is another recycle recipe using the crumbs from freeze dried food. Or you can get prepared dehydrated food like Embark that calls for adding water before serving.

Macaroni and Cheese

Leftover macaroni and cheese
Small cube   Velveeta cheese

Melt the Velveeta in the microwave. Fill the Kong with the macaroni and cheese and pour the Velveeta on top. Let it cool before serving.

Meat Paste

A portion of your dog's normal kibble
1 teaspoon   Meat paste
1 large piece   Banana

Half fill the Kong with kibble and add the meat paste. Use the handle of the spoon to mix the meat paste into the kibble. Add some more kibble, packing it in well, and then plug the large opening with the banana.

Mashed Potato

Instant mashed potatoes
Dog biscuits, crumbled

Combine the potato and biscuit crumbs and fill the Kong.

Notes: You can use leftover mashed potatoes instead of the instant. If you do use instant, make sure there is no salt in it.

This is a good use for any of the biscuits you've made from other recipes that didn't come out quite perfectly!

Peanut Butter Bread

Peanut Butter
Slice of bread

Spread the peanut butter on the bread and fold it. Push it into the Kong. Serve right away or freeze for later.

Peanut Butter Cheese

	Ripe banana
3 tablespoons	Peanut butter
1 slice	Cheese

Combine all of the ingredients and mix well. Fill the Kong and freeze.

Pumpkin

Canned pumpkin (not pie filling)
Sesame or peanut butter

Combine the pumpkin and sesame or peanut butter and fill the Kong. Serve right away or freeze for later.

Rice Cake

Rice cakes, crumbled
Dried fruit
Cream cheese
Plain croutons

Combine all of the ingredients, mix well and fill the Kong.

Rice Yogurt

White rice, cooked, cold
1 tablespoon Fat free yogurt

Combine the rice and yogurt and fill the Kong. Serve right away or freeze for later.

Sweet Potato

	Sweet potato, warm, freshly cooked
	White rice, warm, freshly cooked
1 tablespoon	Peanut butter

Mash the sweet potato and add the rice and peanut butter mixing well. Fill the Kong with the mix and serve right away.

Note: If you would like to freeze the Kong for later, let the rice and sweet potato cool completely before combining them.

Tuna

1 (6 oz.) can	Light tuna, packed in water
2 tablespoons	Non fat yogurt
1/4 cup	Carrot, grated

Combine all of the ingredients, mix well. Fill the Kong and freeze it.

Microwave Treats

These are very quick and easy treats to make. You may need to adjust the cooking time based on the type of microwave you have. Be careful when you take the plate out after cooking, it will be very hot!

Baby Food

3 jars	Baby food, meat or vegetable
1/2 cup	Oat flour

Combine the baby food and oat flour, mixing well. Drop by teaspoonfuls on a wax paper covered paper plate. Flatten the treats with a fork and cover with a second paper plate.

Microwave on high 4-5 minutes.

Broth

2 cups	Whole wheat flour
2/3 cup	Beef or chicken broth
1 large	Egg, lightly beaten
3 tablespoons	Quick cooking oats

Combine the broth and egg. Stir in the flour and mix well. Add the oats and mix well. Knead just enough to work the flour in completely.

Form small, round balls and place them onto a microwave safe plate.

Microwave on high for 10 minutes.

Notes: You can substitute oat flour for the whole wheat. This is the recipe pictured at the start of this section.

Chicken

1 cube	Chicken bouillon
1/2 cup	Hot water
1 cup	All purpose flour
1 1/2 cup	Powdered milk
1 cup	Rolled oats
1/2 cup	Yellow cornmeal
1 teaspoon	Sugar
1/3 cup	Shortening
1	Egg, lightly beaten

Dissolve the bouillon cube in the hot water and set aside.

Combine the dry ingredients, cut in the shortening, then stir in the egg and bouillon. Form the dough into a ball.

Place the ball of dough onto a floured board and knead for 5 minutes until smooth and elastic. Roll the dough out to about 1/2 inch thick. Cut into shapes with a cookie cutter and place on a microwave safe dish.

Microwave at 50% for 5 minutes. Turn the treats over and continue to microwave for another 5 minutes or until firm and dry to the touch.

Cornmeal Beef

1 cup	Whole wheat flour
1/2 cup	All purpose flour
1/4 cup	Cornmeal
3/4 cup	Powdered milk
1/2 cup	Oatmeal, quick cooking
2 tablespoons	Sugar
1/3 cup	Shortening
1 tablespoon	Beef bouillon granules
1	Egg, slightly beaten
1/2 cup	Hot water

Combine the flour, cornmeal, milk, oatmeal and sugar and mix well.

Cut in the shortening. Add the egg, bouillon and hot water.

Place the ball of dough onto a floured board and knead for 5 minutes or until smooth. Roll the dough out to about 1/2 inch thick. Cut into small shapes with a cookie cutter and place the shapes on a microwave safe dish.

Microwave in at 50% power for 5-10 minutes.

Notes: Smaller shapes work better and allow the cookie to cook more evenly. You can substitute chicken bouillon instead of the beef if desired.

Tuna Treats

1	Egg, lightly beaten
1 can	Light tuna in oil, flaked
3/4 cup	Flour

Combine the egg and tuna and mix well. Add the flour a little at a time to form a batter.

Spread the batter evenly on a microwave safe dish.

Microwave on high for up to 6 minutes. 4 minutes will make them more chewy.

Remove the cooked sheet of treats from the plate and cut it up into strips or small squares.

Muffins

Apple Cinnamon

1 1/3 cups	Apple juice
1 large	Egg
2 tablespoons	Vegetable oil
2 tablespoons	Brown sugar
1/2 cup	Apple, chopped
1/2 teaspoon	Salt
1 1/4 cups	Whole wheat flour
1 1/4 cups	All purpose flour
1/2 cup	Oats, uncooked
1/2 teaspoon	Baking soda
2 tablespoons	Dried orange peel or orange zest
1 teaspoon	Cinnamon
2 teaspoons	Rapid or instant yeast

This recipe uses a bread machine, if you don't have one you can mix the ingredients by hand.

Place all of the ingredients in the pan of your bread machine and set on the dough cycle. Turn the machine off after all of the ingredients are mixed well.

Preheat your oven to 350°. Spray mini muffin tins with vegetable oil spray.

Spoon the batter into the mini muffin cups, filling each cup 1/4 full.

Bake for 30 minutes or until a toothpick inserted in the center comes out dry.

Apple Crunch

2 3/4 cups	Water
2 tablespoons	Honey
1/4 cup	Unsweetened applesauce
1/8 teaspoon	Vanilla extract
1 medium	Egg
4 cups	Whole wheat flour
1 cup	Dried apple
1 tablespoon	Baking powder

Preheat your oven to 350°. Spray muffin tins with vegetable oil spray.

Combine the water, honey, applesauce, vanilla and egg in a bowl and mix well.

In another bowl, combine the flour, dried apple and baking powder.

Add the liquid ingredients to the dry and mix well. Pour the batter into the muffin cups.

Bake 1 1/4 hours or until a toothpick inserted in the center comes out dry.

Bacon Cheese

2 cups	Whole wheat flour
1 tablespoon	Baking powder
2 cups	Cheddar cheese, grated
4 slices	Bacon, cooked and crumbled
1 cup	Milk
2	Eggs, slightly beaten
1/4 cup	Vegetable oil

Preheat your oven to 350°. Spray muffin tins with vegetable oil spray.

Combine the flour and baking powder and mix well. Add the grated cheddar cheese and bacon and mix well

In another bowl combine the eggs, milk and vegetable oil mixing well.

Pour the wet ingredients into the dry and mix well.

Spoon the batter into the muffin cups, filling each cup 1/3 full.

Bake for 20-25 minutes or until a toothpick inserted in the center comes out dry.

Note: These can be frozen.

Carrot

2 cups	Carrots, shredded
3	Eggs
1/2 cup	Applesauce, unsweetened
2 teaspoons	Cinnamon
1/2 cup	Rolled oats
3 cups	Whole wheat flour

Preheat your oven to 350°. Spray muffin tins with vegetable oil spray.

Combine the carrots, eggs and applesauce.

In another bowl combine the cinnamon, oats and flour.

Slowly add the dry ingredients to the wet and mix well. Spoon the batter into the muffin cups.

Bake for 25 minutes or until a toothpick inserted in the center comes out dry.

Notes: They will not rise very much, so do not worry about over filling the muffin tins.

You can use one of the frosting recipes from the Icing and Frosting section to spice up these muffins.

They will keep fresh in your refrigerator for 2 weeks. You can freeze them for up to 2 months but wait until you are ready to serve them before frosting.

Fruitcake

1 cup	Fresh cranberries
1	Apple, peeled and cored
1 cup	Pecans
2 cups	All-purpose flour
1/3 cup	Molasses
1	Egg
1 teaspoon	Baking powder
1 teaspoon	Cinnamon
1 cup	Water

Preheat your oven to 350°. Spray mini muffin tins with vegetable oil spray.

Chop the cranberries, apple, and pecans in a food processor or blender.

Combine all of the other ingredients and mix well. Add the chopped fruit and nuts and mix well.

Pour the batter into the muffin cups.

Bake for 30 minutes or until a toothpick inserted in the center comes out dry.

Notes: You can substitute walnuts, almonds or cashews for the pecans if desired.

You can also place an extra nut on top of each muffin for decoration.

Oatmeal Cherry

1 cup	Rolled oats
1 cup	Whole wheat flour
1/2 teaspoon	Cinnamon
3/4 cup	Buttermilk
1	Egg, slightly beaten
1/4 cup	Applesauce, unsweetened
1 cup	Frozen cherries, rinsed and chopped

Preheat your oven to 400°. Spray muffin tins with vegetable oil spray.

Combine the oats, flour, and cinnamon and mix well.

In another bowl, combine the buttermilk, egg and applesauce and mix well.

Combine the wet with the dry ingredients and stir until moist. Add the cherries and mix well.

Spoon the batter into the muffin cups, filling each cup 2/3 full.

Bake for 15-20 minutes or until a toothpick inserted in the center comes out dry.

Note: The cherries do not need to be thawed prior to adding them to the batter.

Peanut

2 tablespoons	Honey
3 cups	Whole-wheat flour
1 cups	All purpose flour
1 tablespoon	Baking powder
1 tablespoon	Cinnamon
1 tablespoon	Nutmeg
2 3/4 cups	Water
1/4 cup	Unsweetened chunky applesauce
1	Egg, slightly beaten
1/2 cup	Peanuts, coarsely chopped

Preheat oven to 350°. Spray muffin tins with vegetable oil spray.

Combine the honey, flour, baking powder, cinnamon and nutmeg and mix well.

Add the water, applesauce and egg and stir, mixing well. Stir in the nuts.

Spoon the batter into the muffin cups, filling each cup 2/3 full.

Bake for 30-35 minutes until lightly browned.

Peanut Butter Banana

1/2 cup	Canola oil
1/2 cup	Applesauce, unsweetened
1/4 cup	Molasses
1/4 cup	Peanut butter
4	Eggs
2 cups	Whole wheat flour
2 teaspoons	Baking soda
2 teaspoons	Cinnamon
2	Bananas, ripe, mashed

Preheat oven to 350°. Spray muffin tins with vegetable oil spray.

Combine the canola oil, applesauce and molasses and mix well with a hand mixer. Add the peanut butter and mix until well combined. Add the eggs one at a time mixing well.

In another bowl combine the flour, baking soda and cinnamon.

Slowly add the dry ingredients to the wet mixing them with the hand mixer on a low speed. Fold in the mashed bananas.

Spoon the batter into the muffin cups.

Bake for 30 minutes or until a toothpick inserted in the center comes out dry.

Squash

1 1/2 cups	Squash, peeled and cubed
1/8 cup	Water
1 cup	Whole wheat flour
1 cup	Oats
1 teaspoon	Ginger
1 teaspoon	Cinnamon
1	Egg
1 tablespoon	Vegetable oil
1/2 cup	Milk

Place the squash and water in a microwave safe bowl and microwave on high at one minute intervals until tender. When soft, drain the squash and let it cool.

Preheat your oven to 375°. Spray muffin tins with vegetable oil spray.

Combine the flour, oats, ginger and cinnamon and mix well.

Combine the cooled squash, egg, oil and milk in a food processor or blender and process until smooth.

Add the squash mixture to the dry mixture and mix well.

Spoon the batter into the muffin cups, filling each cup generously.

Bake for 15 minutes or until a toothpick inserted in the center comes out dry.

Note: This is the recipe pictured at the start of this section.

Recycle Treats

I call them recycle treats because they use the crumbs that are left in the bottom of freeze dried food bags. If you serve your dog freeze dried food you know what I'm talking about! I used to use it for a topping until I discovered these recipes. If you don't normally feed your dog freeze dried food, you can get prepared dehydrated food like Embark and use that or try putting your dog's kibble in a food processor and creating a powder. If you do use your dog's kibble it won't need to be rehydrated.

In these recipes I refer to it as freeze dried food powder and it makes an excellent substitute for flour.

Ground Chicken

2 cups	Freeze dried food powder
1 cup	Hot water
1 cup	Ground chicken
2	Eggs

Preheat your oven to 375°. Spray cookie sheets with vegetable oil spray.

Combine all of the ingredients in a bowl and stir until well mixed. Using a teaspoon or your hands, form small patties and place them on the cookie sheets about 1 inch apart.

Bake for 10 minutes. If desired, turn the oven off and leave the biscuits in for up to 3 hours to make them extra crisp.

Oat

1 cup	Oats
1/4 cup	Nutritional yeast
1/4 cup	Freeze dried food powder
2 large	Eggs
1 tablespoon	Olive oil

Preheat the oven to 350°. Line cookie sheets with wax or parchment paper.

Combine the oats, yeast and food powder and mix well. Add the eggs and oil and mix well.

Using a teaspoon or your hands, form small balls and place them on the cookie sheets.

Bake for 10-15 minutes until lightly browned.

Oat Yogurt

1/3 cup	Freeze dried food powder
1/2 cup	Very hot water
1	Egg
2 tablespoons	Low fat plain yogurt
2 tablespoons	Canola or safflower oil
1 cup	Whole oat flour

Combine the food powder with the water and set aside for 15 minutes to rehydrate it.

Preheat the oven to 400°. Line cookie sheets with wax or parchment paper.

Combine all of the ingredients mixing well. Refrigerate the batter for 30 minutes.

Using a teaspoon or your hands, form small balls and place them on the cookie sheets.

Bake for 7 minutes. If desired, turn the oven off and leave the biscuits in for 45 minutes to 1 hour to make them extra crisp.

Pumpkin (Version 1)

1 cup	Freeze dried food powder
1 cup	Canned pumpkin (not pie filling)
1	Egg
Small handful	Quinoa, buckwheat or oat flour

Preheat your oven to 350°. Spray cookie sheets with vegetable oil spray.

Combine the powder and pumpkin mixing well. Add the egg and flour and mix well. Shape the dough into balls and place them on the cookie sheets.

Bake for 15-20 minutes or until slightly golden and soft inside.

Note: This is the recipe pictured at the start of this section.

Pumpkin (Version 2)

1 cup	Freeze dried food powder
1 cup	Water
1/2 cup	Canned pumpkin
1/4 cup	Quinoa
2 teaspoon	Honey
1	Egg

Combine the food powder with the water and set aside for 15 minutes to rehydrate it.

Preheat the oven to 350°. Spray cookie sheets with vegetable oil spray.

Combine all of the ingredients mixing well. Shape the dough into balls and place them on the cookie sheets.

Bake 20-30 minutes.

Soft Treats

These treats are great for the senior dogs in your household. They are good also for any dogs with issues with their teeth.

Baby Food Meat

2 (2.5 oz.) jars	Baby food meat
1	Egg
1/2 cup	Flour (oat, rice or wheat)
1/4 cup	Parmesan cheese

Preheat your oven to 350°. Spray cookie sheets with vegetable oil spray or line them with parchment paper or non-stick foil.

Combine all of the ingredients and mix well.

Spoon the batter into a pastry bag and squeeze out bite-sized dots of batter onto the cookie sheets. If you don't have a pastry bag you can use a spoon.

Bake for 20 minutes or until they are a light brown and still soft.

Baby Food Vegetarian

1 (4 oz.) jar	Baby food vegetables
6 1/2 teaspoons	Powdered milk
6 1/2 teaspoons	Cream of Wheat

Preheat your oven to 350° and spray cookie sheets with vegetable oil spray.

Combine all of the ingredients and mix well. The batter should be thick enough to form a ball. If it's too thin, add equal amounts of extra powdered milk and Cream of Wheat. Let the batter sit at room temperature for 10-15 minutes.

Form the dough into small balls and place them on the cookie sheets. Press the balls flat with the tines of a fork.

Bake for 15 minutes.

Banana Applesauce

1	Ripe banana, mashed
1 cup	Carrot, shredded
1/4 cup	Applesauce, unsweetened
1/8 cup	Water
1 cup	Oats
1 1/2 cups	Whole wheat flour

Preheat your oven to 350° and spray cookie sheets with vegetable oil spray.

Combine the banana and carrot and mix well. Add the applesauce and water and mix well.

Add the oats and mix well. Add the flour a little at a time to form a soft dough.

Place the dough onto a floured board and roll out to 1/2 inch thick. Cut into shapes with a cookie cutter and place on the cookie sheets.

Bake for 25 minutes. Turn the oven off and let them sit inside for up to 3 hours to create a chewy texture.

Chicken (Version 1)

2 cubes	Chicken bouillon
1 cup	Boiling water
1/2 cup	Vegetable oil
2	Eggs, beaten
2 cups	Whole wheat flour
1/2 cup	Cornmeal, stone ground
1 1/2 cups	Powdered skim milk
1 cup	Quick cooking rolled oats

Dissolve the bouillon in the boiling water and set aside until at room temperature. When at room temperature, add the vegetable oil and eggs, mixing well.

Combine the flour, cornmeal, powdered milk and oats and mix well.

Add the wet ingredients to the dry and mix well.

Place the dough onto a floured board and knead for 4-5 minutes. Roll the dough out to 1/2 inch thick, cut into shapes with a cookie cutter and place on a microwave safe plate.

Microwave on medium for 5 minutes. Turn each biscuit over and microwave for another 5 minutes. Turn them again and microwave another 2-5 minutes.

Chicken (Version 2)

1 package	Active dry yeast
Pinch	White sugar
1/4 cup	Warm water
2 cubes	Chicken bouillon
4 cups	Boiling water
3 1/2 cups	All purpose flour
1 1/2 cups	Whole wheat flour
1 1/2 cups	Rye flour
1 cup	Cornmeal
1/2 cup	Powdered skim milk

Dissolve the yeast and sugar in the warm water and set aside.

In another bowl, dissolve the bouillon in the boiling water and set aside until at room temperature.

Preheat your oven to 300° and spray cookie sheets with vegetable oil spray.

Combine flour, cornmeal, and powdered milk and mix well. Combine the yeast and bouillon mixtures and mix well. Slowly stir the wet ingredients into the dry mixing well.

Place the dough onto a floured board and knead for 1 minute. Roll the dough out to 1/2 inch thick, cut into shapes with a cookie cutter and place on the cookie sheets.

Bake for 25 minutes. Remove them from the oven and turn each biscuit over. Continue baking for another 25 minutes.

Peanut Butter Pumpkin

1/2 cup	Peanut butter
1 cup	Canned pumpkin (not pie filling)
1/2 teaspoon	Cinnamon
1 3/4 cups	Oat flour

Preheat your oven to 350° and line cookie sheets with parchment paper.

Combine the peanut butter, pumpkin and cinnamon and mix well.

Add the flour a little at a time to form a dough that is not sticky. If it is too sticky to roll out, add a little more flour.

Roll the dough out between two sheets of parchment paper or on a floured board to 1/4 inch thick. Cut into shapes with a cookie cutter and place on the cookie sheets.

Bake for 8 minutes.

Pumpkin

1 1/4 cup	Canned pumpkin (not pie filling)
2	Eggs, slightly beaten
2 cups	Whole wheat flour
1 cup	Rolled oats
1/2 teaspoon	Cinnamon
1/2 teaspoon	Ground ginger

Preheat your oven to 350° and line cookie sheets with parchment paper.

Combine the pumpkin and eggs and mix well. Add the flour, oats, cinnamon and ginger and mix well.

Using your hands create small balls from the dough and place them on the cookie sheets.

Bake for 20-30 minutes or until a golden brown.

Liver

1 1/2 pounds	Liver, minced
1 cup	Oat flour
2	Eggs
1 teaspoon	Garlic powder (optional)

Preheat your oven to 350° and spray a square cake pan with vegetable oil spray.

Combine all of the ingredients and mix well. Press flat into the cake pan.

Bake for 30 minutes. Cool, remove from pan and cut into small squares.

Note: These treats can be frozen.

Training Treats

Bacon

1 (8.5 oz.) box	Corn muffin mix
Pinch	Garlic powder
1/4 cup	Oats
1/2 teaspoon	Baking soda
4 tablespoons	Bacon, cooked, crumbled
1/2 cup	Beef bouillon
1/4-1/2 cup	All purpose flour

Preheat your oven to 350°.

Combine the muffin mix, garlic powder, oats and baking soda and mix well. Add the bacon and mix well. Add the bouillon and mix well. Add the flour a little at a time to form a dough.

Spoon the dough in small, treat-sized balls onto cookie sheets.

Bake for 10-14 minutes or until they are golden brown.

Chicken Tuna

1 can	White chicken in water, drained
1 can	Tuna in water, drained
1 can	Garbanzo beans, rinsed and drained well
2	Eggs
1/2 cup	Quick oats (optional)

Preheat your oven to 200° and spray a cookie sheet with vegetable oil spray.

Combine all of the ingredients in a food processor or blender and process until mixed well.

Spread the batter out on the cookie sheets to 1/4 inch thickness.

Bake for 4-6 hours, turning them over half way through. Bake until fully dehydrated.

Cut the treats into small training sized pieces.

Note: These are the treats pictured at the start of this section.

Peanut Butter

4 cups	Garbanzo bean flour
1/2 cup	Ground flax seed
1 cup	Peanut butter
1 cup	Applesauce, unsweetened
1/4 cup	Vegetable oil
1 cup	Water

Preheat your oven to 350° and spray a cookie sheet with vegetable oil spray.

Combine the flour and flax seed and mix well. Combine the rest of the ingredients and mix well.

Add the wet ingredients to the dry, mixing well.

Spread the batter on the cookie sheet.

Bake for 30 minutes. Let the treats cool and cut into training sized pieces.

Salmon

1 (14.75 oz.) can	Pink Salmon, do not drain
2	Eggs
2 cups	All purpose flour

Preheat your oven to 350° and spray a cookie sheet with vegetable oil spray.

Combine the salmon and liquid with the eggs and mix well. Add the flour and mix well.

Spread the batter on the cookie sheet to 1/4 inch thickness.

Bake for 25-35 minutes, depending on whether you want softer or crunchier treats.

Let the treats cool and cut into training sized pieces.

Tuna Squares

2 cans	Tuna, in water, drained
2	Eggs
1 teaspoon	Garlic powder
1 1/2 cups	All purpose Flour

Preheat your oven to 250° and spray a cookie sheet with vegetable oil spray.

Combine all of the ingredients and mix well. Spread the batter on the cookie sheet to 1/4 inch thickness.

Bake for 30 minutes. Let the treats cool and cut into training sized pieces.

Note: These treats can be frozen.

Bonus Section – Health Conscious Biscuits

Dental

These treats are specifically for your dog's teeth and gum health. You can use any cookie cutter for the recipes, but toothbrush shaped cutters make them more fun.

Honey Peppermint

1/4 cup	Honey
1 1/2 cups	Whole wheat flour
1 cup	All purpose flour
1/2 cup	Cornmeal
1/4 cup	Spinach powder
1/2 cup	Oats
1/4 cup	Bran
1 tablespoon	Bone meal
1 1/2 teaspoons	Baking powder
1 1/2 cups	Water
1 teaspoon	Peppermint extract

Preheat your oven to 350° and spray cookie sheets with vegetable oil spray.

Combine all of the ingredients and mix well. You can use your bread machine on the dough cycle if you want. Remove the dough when it is completely mixed.

Place the dough onto a floured board roll out to 1/4 inch thick, cut into shapes with a cookie cutter and place on the cookie sheets.

Bake for about 45 minutes until golden brown. Turn the oven off and leave them in the oven for several hours or overnight to harden. You want them to be very hard to help remove built-up tartar on your dog's teeth.

Maple Mint

1 1/2 cups	Whole wheat flour
1 1/2 cups	Bisquick baking mix
1/2 cup	Mint leaves
1/4 cup	Milk
4 tablespoons	Margarine
1	Egg
1 1/2 tablespoons	Maple syrup

Preheat your oven to 375° and spray cookie sheets with vegetable oil spray.

Combine all of the ingredients in food processor or blender and process until well mixed and a dough ball forms.

Place the dough onto a floured board roll out to 1/4 inch thick, cut into shapes with a cookie cutter and place on the cookie sheets.

Bake for 20 minutes or until lightly browned.

Note: You can substitute corn syrup for the maple if desired.

Mint

2 cups	Brown rice flour
3 tablespoons	Canola or vegetable oil
1	Egg
1/2 cup	Fresh mint, chopped
1/2 cup	Fresh parsley, chopped
2/3 cup	Low fat milk

Preheat your oven to 400° and spray cookie sheets with vegetable oil spray.

Combine all of the ingredients and mix well.

Using a teaspoon, drop the dough in small balls on the cookie sheets.

Bake for 15-20 minutes or until golden brown.

Wheat

3/4 cup	Powdered skim milk
1/2 cup	Cornmeal
1/4 cup	Bulgur wheat
2 1/4 cups	Whole wheat flour
1 cube	Chicken bouillon
1 1/2 cups	Boiling water
1 cup	Rolled oats, quick cooking
1	Egg, slightly beaten

Preheat your oven to 325° and spray cookie sheets with vegetable oil spray.

Combine the powdered milk, cornmeal, bulgur and flour and mix well.

In another bowl, dissolve the bouillon cube in the boiling water. Add the oats and let it stand for 5 minutes. Add the egg and mix well.

Add the dry ingredients to the wet a little at a time, mixing well.

Place the dough onto a floured board and knead for about 5 minutes. Roll the dough out to 1/4 inch thick, cut into shapes with a cookie cutter and place on the cookie sheets.

Bake for 50 minutes. Turn the oven off and leave them in the oven for several hours or overnight to harden. You want them to be very hard to help remove built-up tartar on your dog's teeth.

Flea Repellant

Garlic Beef

2 cubes	Beef bouillon
1 3/4 cups	Boiling water
1/2 cup	Vegetable oil
1	Egg, beaten
1 1/2 cups	All purpose flour
1 1/2 cups	Whole wheat flour
1 cup	Rye flour
1 cup	Quick cooking oats
1 cup	Cornmeal
1/4 cup	Brewers yeast
2 tablespoons	Garlic powder

Dissolve the bouillon cubes in the boiling water and set aside to cool. When it's cool, add the oil and egg and mix well.

Preheat your oven to 300° and spray cookie sheets with vegetable oil spray.

Combine the flours, oats, cornmeal, yeast and garlic powder. Slowly add the wet ingredients and mix well.

Place the dough onto a floured board and knead for about 3-4 minutes. Roll the dough out to 1/4 inch thick, cut into shapes with a cookie cutter and place on the cookie sheets.

Bake for 1 1/2 hours until hard.

Garlic Chicken (Version 1)

1 cup	Flour
1/4 cup	Wheat germ
1/4 cup	Brewers yeast
1 teaspoon	Salt
2 tablespoons	Vegetable oil
1 teaspoon	Garlic powder (optional)
1/2 cup	Chicken stock

Preheat your oven to 400° and spray cookie sheets with vegetable oil spray or line them with parchment paper.

Combine the flour, wheat germ, Brewers yeast, and salt and mix well.

Combine the oil, garlic and chicken stock, mixing well.

Slowly add the wet ingredients to the dry and mix well.

Place the dough onto a floured board and knead for about 2 minutes. Roll the dough out to 1/4 inch thick, cut into shapes with a cookie cutter and place on the cookie sheets.

Bake for 20 minutes. Turn the oven off and leave them in the oven for 1-2 hours to harden.

Garlic Chicken (Version 2)

2 cups	Flour
1/2 cup	Wheat germ
1/2 cup	Brewers yeast
1 teaspoon	Salt
2 cloves	Garlic, minced
3 tablespoons	Vegetable oil
1 cup	Chicken stock

Preheat your oven to 400° and spray cookie sheets with vegetable oil spray or line them with parchment paper.

Combine flour, wheat germ, Brewers yeast and salt and mix well.

In another bowl, combine the garlic and oil. Slowly stir the dry ingredients and stock alternately into the wet ingredients, mixing well to form a soft dough ball.

Place the dough onto a floured board and roll it out to 1/2 inch thick, cut into shapes with a cookie cutter and place on the cookie sheets.

Bake 20-25 minutes or until well-browned. Turn the oven off and leave them in the oven for 1-3 hours to harden.

About the Author

Cathy L. Kidd is a craftsperson at heart. For as long as she can remember she has been creating things with her hands. She has done crochet (taught to her by her Aunt Carol), stained glass (learned by taking a class), candlemaking (learned from an ebook) and cooking (learned initially from Betty Crocker!)

Her other homemade recipe books include:
Homemade Bread Recipes – A Simple and Easy Bread Machine Cookbook

How to Make Homemade Bread – Simple and Easy Bread Making Tips and Recipes

Homemade Soup Recipes: Simple and Easy Slow Cooker Recipes

How to Make Homemade Ice Cream: Simple and Easy Ice Cream Maker Recipes

How to Make Smoothies: Simple, Easy and Healthy Blender Recipes

Dehydrating Food: Simple and Easy Dehydrator Recipes

For more recipes visit: www.easyhomemadebreadrecipes.com and join us on Facebook at https://www.facebook.com/RecipesForYourKitchenAppliances

For color photos, links to some of the products mentioned in this book and to download a bonus, printable pdf of the recipes pictured in this book, go to: http://luiniunlimitedpublications.com/?p=107

Printed in Great Britain
by Amazon